Healthcare And Technology Today:

A Guide for Providers and Practice
Managers

Healthcare And Technology Today: A Guide for Providers and
Practice Managers

Adam Levy

For the last six years, Adam Levy has been the owner of Magnet Solutions Group (MagnetSolutionsGroup.com), an IT services and web development firm located in Austin, TX. Magnet Solutions Group works with businesses of all types in Central Texas and throughout the United States.

When he is not working, he enjoys playing hockey and exploring Texas with his wife Erika--while trying as much great BBQ as they can.

Adam is also a frequent speaker on IT topics for business owners and managers.

Adam can be reached by email at Adam@MagnetSolutionsGroup.com.

Healthcare And Technology Today: A Guide for Providers and
Practice Managers

Table of Contents

Healthcare And Technology Today: A Guide for Providers and
Practice Managers

Introduction

There has perhaps been no industry in
history that has received more legislative and
media attention about its technology use than the
healthcare industry in the last decade or so. The
topic of Healthcare IT (HIT) has intersected with
some of the major news and legislation stories of
our times--from the HITECH Act of 2009, which
was part of the Congressional response to the
worst economic crisis of our generation, to the
constant discussions about controlling healthcare
costs and improving patient care that came with
the proposal and passage of The Patient
Protection and Affordable Care Act
("Obamacare"), to the seemingly never-ending
revelations of consumer information hacks and
data security threats across all industries, to the
constantly referenced (but very frequently mis-
understood) HIPAA legislation. Even the
challenges with the launching of the
healthcare.gov insurance enrollment website
created national headlines and discussion. It can
make one wonder: how can the use of computers

by one industry possibly generate so much
concern in the general public and in government?

The answer seems to be related to six key facts.
First, the size of the healthcare industry. When all
healthcare-related spending is accounted for,
healthcare in the United States accounts for about
1/6 of our national GDP. Spending on healthcare
roughly equals total annual federal government
expenditures.

Second, the healthcare industry has a uniquely
trusting relationship with the people it serves.
Maintaining the privacy of the information shared
between doctor and patient is hugely important.
This raises strong and legitimate concerns about
access controls to electronic patient health
information (ePHI).

Third, alongside the desire for maintaining
privacy, there is a strong desire among many
patients and doctors for better, more efficient
access to patient information and medical
histories. In particular, many patients (especially
those dealing with ongoing health issues) today
find it very burdensome to keep track of their
records as they deal with multiple specialists and
providers.

Fourth, healthcare is fairly unique in the ability of
incorrect information to lead to errors that
significantly harm individuals. It does not require
too much effort to imagine a scenario in which a

doctor accesses incorrect electronic medicine allergy information for a patient and writes a harmful prescription.

Fifth, since the industry is so data-intensive, from patient medical information, to educational materials, to billing and scheduling information, the potential for better use of computers presents exciting possibilities for improved care and reduced costs over time.

Finally, as anyone who has been involved with healthcare IT knows, the healthcare industry is incredibly complex and designing IT solutions that serve everybody's needs well is just *really hard*.

The Purpose of This Book

With a topic getting this much attention, there's obviously a ton of information out there about HIT. Probably more than any one person could ever read. The point of this book is not to re-cover all of that information or to turn the reader into an information technology expert. This book is designed to provide a short, useful introduction to healthcare information technology today and how it applies to medical practices. We hope that practice managers and providers (as well as others working in medical practices) will find it to be a valuable guide that gives a basis of understanding of the topic that can be read in a sitting or two and kept on hand as a quick reference.

Two notes on our intended audience. First, this book isn't a technical guide and it's not written for IT technicians. Those resources exist elsewhere. Second, this book isn't intended to address IT at large institutions or hospitals. Though there is overlap obviously with some of the ideas presented here, those facilities generally have different needs—and resources—when it comes to information technology.

Ch. 1: An Overview of Healthcare IT
Legislation

As we noted in the introduction, healthcare
IT has been the focus of legislators for several
years. From HIPAA to HITECH, there are a lot of
acronyms involved and things can get confusing
quickly. There are also several government bodies
and agencies and administrative positions
involved in governing HIT—which are also an
alphabet soup of acronyms that we'll sort out.
This chapter is designed to give an overview of
the legislation and government agencies (as well
as three important nonprofit agencies) that are
shaping HIT.

A role for the federal government in promoting HIT
advancement—and in particular, the use of
electronic health records (EHR) that can be
shared easily among providers in different
locations—has been advocated by both major
political parties over the last few decades.

Through an executive order in 1997, Bill Clinton
established the President's Information
Technology Advisory Committee (PITAC). In

describing the importance of PITAC, President Clinton noted in particular the importance of IT in healthcare:

"Half of our economic productivity in the last half century is attributable to science and technological innovation. One third of our economic growth since 1992 has been spurred by businesses in the computing and communications industries. Information technology sustains our global competitiveness, provides opportunities for lifelong learning, and expands our ability to solve critical problems affecting our environment, health care and national security.

In his inauguration address of George W. Bush in 2004 included a call for electronic health records:

"By computerizing health records, we can avoid dangerous medical mistakes, reduce costs, and improve care."

And as President-Elect in 2009, Barack Obama also called for electronic health records:

"To improve the quality of our health care while lowering its cost, we will make the immediate investments necessary to ensure that, within five years, all of America's medical records are computerized. This will cut waste, eliminate red tape and reduce the need to repeat expensive medical tests."

The attraction of promoting healthcare IT—and in particular the use of electronic health records—primarily because of the possibilities of improved patient safety and significant savings has proven to be something neither party can resist promoting.

So, with this political background, what are the policies that have been enacted that affect healthcare IT, why have they been enacted, and what do they mean for providers today?

HIPAA

A good place to start is with the passage of The Health Insurance Portability and Accountability Act (HIPAA) in 1996. HIPAA was an attempt to legislate a standard set of guidelines for protecting patient information while facilitating increased sharing of patient information. Such guidelines had not had existed before in the healthcare industry. Among other factors, HIPAA was spurred by the fact that the healthcare industry was already starting to transition to more frequent use of electronic records and by the fact that there was an increased need for sharing records more efficiently—among different providers and specialists working with the same patient, among insurance companies dealing with claims and among insurance companies dealing with

eligibility questions. HIPAA directed the US
Department of Health and Human Services (HHS)
to develop regulations on these issues. HHS
responded by publishing The HIPAA Privacy Rule
and the HIPAA Security Rule.

The HIPAA Privacy Rule

  The HIPAA Privacy Rule went into effect on
April 14, 2003. The HIPAA Privacy Rule deals
with protecting the privacy of individually
identifiable health information, including medical
records—protected health information (PHI). The
Privacy Rule requires that all organizations
covered by the rule (known as 'covered entities'
and including healthcare providers, health plans
and health care clearinghouses) enact safeguards
to protect this patient information and impose
limits on sharing it without patient authorization.
(We'll talk more about these requirements in our
later chapter on HIPAA.)   The Privacy Rule also
gives patients the right to obtain a copy of their
health records and to request corrections to the
records.

The HIPAA Security Rule

  The HIPAA Security Rule went into effect
on April 21, 2003. Compliance for most covered

entities was required by April 21, 2005. While the
Privacy Rule covers all protected health
information (PHI), the Security Rule specifically
deals with electronic protected health information
(ePHI). The stated motivation for the Security
Rule was to address the need for safeguards
(both physical and technical) around the electronic
transmission of patient data while also ensuring
that these safeguards did not restrict the growth of
electronic records in the healthcare industry.
We'll address these provisions in our later chapter
on HIPAA.

The HITECH Act

Following the financial crisis and economic
downturn of 2008, the federal government
responded by enacting a 'stimulus package',
known officially as the American Recovery and
Reinvestment Act (ARRA). ARRA was signed into
law in February 2009. Of the $789 billion in
government spending allocated in the bill, $147
billion was directed toward the healthcare
industry. This portion of ARRA dealing with
healthcare is known as the Health Information
Technology for Economic and Clinical Health Act
(HITECH).

Meaningful Use

There has been no single piece of legislation that has had a greater impact in spurring the adoption of healthcare IT in the United States than the HITECH Act. The primary reason for this profound effect is that the HITECH Act allocated $19 billion in funds to hospitals and providers as incentives for adopting healthcare technology that is used in a 'meaningful' way. 'Meaningful Use' has become the shorthand term in healthcare to refer to this incentive program. The program is run through the Centers for Medicare and Medicaid Services (CMS) and is formally known as the Medicare and Medicaid EHR Incentive Programs. A number of statistics point to the significant increase in investment by the healthcare industry in the years following adoption of the legislation.

Recognizing the significant cost and effort involved in transitioning to electronic records, Meaningful Use was designed to be implemented through a series of three phases over the course of five years. Each phase has specific requirements that need to be met in order to qualify for achieving 'Meaningful Use.' Those hospitals and providers that do meet these criteria and that receive federal Medicare and Medicaid funds are eligible to receive incentive funds, which can range into the tens of thousands of dollars.

Strengthening of HIPAA

Besides launching the meaningful use incentive program, the HITECH Act also further strengthened some of the privacy controls of HIPAA. This was done because the writers of the HITECH Act obviously knew that their legislation would lead to a huge increase in the exchange of ePHI and felt more safeguards for privacy would be needed. Perhaps another reason for the strengthening of privacy controls was public expectation. If practices are to receive federal taxpayer dollars to invest in more technology, there is an increased expectation that those technologies are secure and used appropriately.

Previously, HIPAA was not regularly or strongly enforced by regulators. The HITECH Act provides for mandatory penalties for 'willful neglect.' We'll address this in more detail in the later chapter on HIPAA compliance, but generally speaking, willful neglect means that providers have made no effort or such a cursory, non-significant effort at privacy compliance that they can't really say with a straight face that their efforts reflect a genuine concern with compliance. Civil penalties were increased and criminal penalties mandated for certain activities. And the legislation also requires the HHS to conduct regular audits of covered entities.

The HITECH Act also now makes certain HIPAA requirements—and certain civil and criminal liability--directly applicable to business associates of covered entities. The law now requires business associates to report security breaches to covered entities. As a notable example, most (fi not all) software vendors providing EHR solutions are considered business associates.

The HITECH Act also requires providers to notify patients in case of data breaches and to notify the Department of Health and Human Services in cases where data breaches affect more than 500 patients. The law also requires that practices be able to provide a copy of a patient's electronic medical record when requested.

ICD-10 Final Rule

On January 16, 2009 CMS issued a final rule requiring all HIPAA covered entities to transition to the International Statistical Classification of Diseases and Related Health Problems: Tenth Revision (ICD-10) by October 2013. That compliance date was later extended to October 1, 2015.

The motivation behind this mandate is to have a coding system with more breadth and detail that can also support interoperability internationally.

Although ICD-10 is not part of the HIPAA Security and Privacy Rules, entities that fail to use this coding system for procedures and diagnoses occurring after October 1, 2015 are considered in breach of HIPAA. EHR software providers were required to update their software to work with ICD-10 in order to maintain meaningful use certification.

MACRA

In 2015, Congress passed the Medicare Access and CHIP Reauthorization Act of 2015 (MACRA), which focuses more on quality of care versus quantity of care in incentive payments. MACRA's Merit Based Incentive Payments System (MIPS) reimbursement payments will go into effect in 2019 and will increase compensation to eligible providers for positive incomes and reduce compensation for negative outcomes.

Government Agencies

As HIT becomes a bigger and bigger part of healthcare delivery, it's useful to have some familiarity with the government agencies and committees that are driving HIT policy. Though responsibility for HIT in different ways reaches across a large number of government agencies, the ones listed here have primary responsibility for defining policies, enactment and enforcement and are the names you'll most frequently come across as you deal with HIT.

CMS

The Centers for Medicare & Medicaid Services (CMS) is part of the Department of Health and Human Services (HHS). CMS administers Medicare, Medicaid and the Children's Health Insurance Program (CHIP). As we noted earlier, CMS runs the Medicare and Medicaid EHR Incentive Programs, better known as 'Meaningful Use.' (CMS also runs the Health Insurance Marketplace.) CMS covers over 100 million patients in the US and its benefits program and their design are a key driver in defining how healthcare IT is implemented in the US.

ONC

The Office of the National Coordinator for Health Information Technology (ONC) is the lead government office for promoting and defining HIT adoption in the United States as well as promoting and defining the electronic exchange of health information. The ONC is located in the Office of the Secretary for the US Department of Health and Human Services (HHS) and was created by an executive order issued by President Bush in

2004. The Office of National Coordinator was
later legislated by the HITECH Act, which gave it
additional funding and responsibilities.

As part of leading implementation and adoption of
HIT, ONC provides the funding for the
development of the Nationwide Health Information
Network (NwHIN)— which is a set of standards,
services and policies that enable the secure
exchange of health information online. (Even
though NwHIN sounds like a physical network or
database, it's not.)

On September 21, 2015 ONC issued the Federal
Health IT Strategic Plan 2015-2020, which
outlines the role of all government agencies
involved in HIT over these five years.

'ONC' is an acronym that you will come across
frequently in discussions of HIT.

HITPC

        The Health IT Policy Committee (HITPC)
was established by the HITECH Act and is under
the control of ONC. The role of the HITPC is to
make recommendations to ONC on a policy
framework for developing and adopting a national
infrastructure for exchanging health information.
Seven working groups, consisting of twenty
members (plus additional members appointed by

the President), make recommendations on
meaningful use of EHRs, certification and
adoption of EHRs, information exchange, NwHIN,
the strategic plan framework, privacy and security
policy and enrollment in federal and state health
and human services programs.

HITSC

The Health IT Standards Committee
(HITSC) was also established by the HITECH ACT
and is under the control of ONC. The role of the
Standards Committee is to make
recommendations to ONC on standards,
implementation specifications and certification
criteria in the use and exchange of healthcare
information. The Standards Committee has four
working groups that deal with clinical operations,
clinical quality, privacy and security, and
implementation strategies to speed up adoption.
HITSC also coordinates the necessary testing for
standards and policy development through the
National Institute of Standards and Technology
(NIST).

NCVHS

The National Committee On Vital and
Health Statistics (NCVHS) was established in

1949 to advise the Secretary of Health and
Human Services on health information policy,
tackling data issues in community and population
health, standards, privacy and confidentiality,
quality and data access and use. In 1996, it was
expanded to deal with issues relating to HIPAA
and it reports regularly to Congress on HIPAA
implementation.

NQF

The National Quality Forum (NQF) is a
nonpartisan nonprofit organization made up of
over 430 member organizations, representing
consumers, health plans, medical professionals,
device manufacturers and government agencies.
It was started in 1999 based on the
recommendation of the President's Advisory
Commission on Consumer Protection and Quality
in the Health Care Industry. The goal of NQF is
improve the quality of healthcare in the United
States by setting performance improvement
priorities and promoting reporting standards and
education related to those priorities. As it relates
to HIT, NQF has been involved in defining
standards for meaningful use.

HIMSS

Healthcare Information and Management Systems Society (HIMSS) is a global nonprofit that was started at the Georgia Institute of Technology in 1961 and is now based in Chicago. HIMSS has a simple vision: 'Better health through information technology.' HIMSS North America has over 64,000 members. HIMSS is a leading resource for thought leadership and education on HIT. HIMSS also sponsors National Health IT Week—yes, HIT has its own week.

AHIMA

The American Health Information Management Association (AHIMA) is a nonprofit organization made up of over 53,000 members. AHIMA was founded in 1928 with the goal of improving record quality in the health profession. Today, AHIMA plays a leading role in pushing the adoption of EHRs.

Ch. 2 Meaningful Use and MACRA

Meaningful Use refers to the overall standard for reimbursement under the Medicare and Medicaid EHR Incentive Programs. As in, 'Is the practice's installed technology being 'meaningfully used?' Since the passage of the HITECH Act in 2009, which is where the term first appeared, 'Meaningful Use' has come to not only be the shorthand name that everybody uses for the Incentive Programs but also the name people use to quickly refer to healthcare IT overall in the United States. As we noted in the introduction, designing successful implementations of healthcare IT has historically been difficult and costly. The idea behind the incentive program mandated in the HITECH Act is to encourage eligible professionals and eligible hospitals to adopt, implement and upgrade (AIU) certified EHRs.

According to CMS, the idea of Meaningful Use is based on achieving 5 priorities:

1. Improving quality, safety, efficiency, and reducing health disparities
2. Engaging patients and families in their health
3. Improving care coordination
4. Improving population and public health
5. Ensuring adequate privacy and security protection for personal health information

An important note here is that the concept of prioritizing meaningful use was a response to the fact that so much HIT that had previously been invested in had not been utilized. The EHR Incentive Programs are intended to make actual *meaningful use*, as it's progressively defined by CMS, the standard for receiving incentives. The EHR Incentive Programs are not reimbursement programs just for purchasing an EHR.

With the idea of avoiding imposing undue hardship or unrealistic deadlines all at once, the HITECH Act mandated a phased approach consisting of three stages. CMS has had the responsibility for defining what constitutes Meaningful Use at each of these stages. The program and its standards and reporting requirements for its three stages include a considerable amount of detail. In fact, CMS has acknowledged that the current reporting and standards regime for Meaningful Use is too burdensome and wastes valuable time and resources of providers. That being said, this chapter will not be a comprehensive list of every

requirement for each phase, but rather an
overview of the requirements and intended goals.
Because Meaningful Use is tied to EHR
implementation and requires approved reporting
features in EHRs for record keeping on
Meaningful Use attainment, any reputable EHR
vendor should help you in setting up your EHR
use so as to be meeting your Meaningful Use
requirements. To receive an incentive payment,
you must use an EHR that is certified specifically
for the EHR Incentive Programs. The possible
incentive payments range from $43,720 over 5
years for Medicare providers and $63,750 over 6
years for Medicaid providers (starting in 2011).

Stage 1/Modified Stage 2/Stage 2

Since October 2015, Stage 1 has been replaced
for new enrollees with Modified Stage 2 objectives
and requirements. The 13 core and 9 optional (or
'menu') requirements that were required of
providers in Stage 1 have been changed to the 10
objectives of Stage 2 and their related specific
requirements to achieve them. Those 10
objectives are:

1. Patient Health Information
2. Clinical Decision Support (CDS)
3. Computerized Provider Order Entry (CPOE)
4. Electronic Prescribing (eRX)
5. Health Information Exchange (HIE)

6. Patient-Specific Education
7. Medication Reconciliation
8. Patient Electronic Access (VDT)
9. Secure Messaging
10. Public Health

Note that for Modified Stage 2 participants,
Objectives 5 and 9 are not required.

Stage 3

CMS also issued its Stage 3 requirements in
October 2015. Stage 3 will begin as optional in
2017 and will be required starting in 2018. There
are 8 objectives for Stage 3:

1. Protected Patient Health Information
2. Electronic Prescribing (eRX)
3. Clinical Decision Support (CDS)
4. Computerized Provider Order Entry (CPOE)
5. Patient Electronic Access to Health
   Information
6. Coordination of Care Through Patient
   Engagement
7. Health Information Exchange (HIE)
8. Public Health and Clinical Data Registry
   Reporting

Clinical Quality Measures

Clinical Quality Measures (CQM) are standards that aim to measure the quality of care provided. CQMs fall into six National Quality Strategy (NQS) categories:

1. Patient and Family Engagement
2. Efficient Use of Healthcare Resources
3. Clinical Processes and Effectiveness
4. Patient Safety
5. Population and Public Health
6. Care Coordination

Starting in 2015, providers must attest to nine CQMs that fall into at least 3 of the 6 NQS categories. CMS has a recommended core of CQMs for pediatric and adult practices. To participate in the Incentive Programs, providers are required to submit CQM data from certified EHR technology. EHRs will allow direct reporting of CQMs to CMS for Medicare participants. Medicaid EHR Incentive Program participants must submit CQM data to their state.

MACRA

The Medicare Access and CHIP Reauthorization Act (MACRA) became law in 2015. MACRA applies to providers covered under

Medicare Part B—it repeals the Medicare Part B
Sustainable Growth Rate (SGR) reimbursement
formula and replaces it with the new Quality
Payment Program (QPP). The idea behind this
change is to align reimbursement for providers
more closely with high quality outcomes. QPP has
two tracks, one of which is the Merit-based
Incentive Payment System (MIPS). Most Part B
providers will be covered by MIPS.

MIPS brings together performance measures from
Meaningful Use, the Physician Quality Reporting
System (PQRS) and the Value-based Payment
Modifier (VPM). Under MIPS, providers will re-
imbursed based on Quality (50%), Resource Use
(10%), Clinical Practice Improvement (15%) and
Meaningful Use of EHR technology (25%). Based
on this composite measurement, providers will
see their re-imbursements adjusted either up or
down (or not at all). Performance for MIPS is
scheduled to begin on January 1, 2017. The
annual MIPS score (0-100) of a practice can
positively or negatively (or neutrally) affect its
reimbursement payments.

Under this new measuring regime, Meaningful
Use becomes one piece of the performance
review. MACRA lets us see that the future of
technology implementations likely will include
focus on interoperability (the successful sharing of
data between systems) and quality patient
outcomes.

Ch.3 EHRs

Let's start this chapter with a point about
paper, in all its majesty. Paper patient records
aren't ideal for sharing among several specialists.
They're obviously not great for easily and
automatically pulling aggregated statistics from
lots of different patients. But paper records are
fantastic for allowing doctors and staff to quickly
make custom notations that make sense to the
people working in a single practice. Paper forms
also allow easy customization of fields based on a
particular practice's needs. Paper records are
also easily flipped through and scanned. Paper
records can be physically locked away in a single
location. These benefits are not easily replaced
by electronic records. It's too easy to say
computers and software are better at everything;
actually designing electronic medical records that
bring the benefits of paper records in terms of
ease-of-use and security is difficult. EHRs are
getting better and satisfaction rates among

providers seems to be rising, although challenges and frustration obviously remain.

Electronic Health Record (EHR) and Electronic Medical Record (EMR) are often used inter-changeably. EHR more specifically refers to software that allows interoperable information exchange across organizations and that is the term we'll use in this chapter.

EHR Certification

The Office of the National Coordinator for Health Information Technology (ONC) Health IT Certification Program is responsible for certifying HIT, including EHRs. ONC works with several designated labs and testing outfits to conduct certification reviews. It's a voluntary program, but any EHR that wishes to be used successfully for Meaningful Use requirements must be certified. You should not invest in any EHR that is not ONC-HIT certified.

Major Features

Stage 2 of Meaningful Use has the following ten core objectives. EHR software is primarily responsible for addressing 9 of these objectives and is partially responsible for the first objective, related to protecting ePHI in accordance with HIPAA requirements. This is important to note; EHR software is critical in achieving (and documenting and reporting) Meaningful Use. Any reputable EHR vendor will work with you to make sure your software is supporting your Meaningful Use requirements.

1.PHI

2.Clinical Decision Support (CDS)

3.CPOE Computerized Provider Order Entry

4. e-Prescribing

5. Health Information Exchange

6. Patient Specific Education

7. Medication Reconciliation

8. Patient Electronic Access

9. Secure Messaging

10. Public Health

Let's look at a few of these Meaningful Use objectives, which translate into major features of any ONC-HIT certified EHR.

CPOE

Computerized Physician Order Entry (CPOE) allows providers to enter medical instructions and treatment orders directly into their EHR. Along with e-Prescribing, the motive here is to reduce preventable errors. Often embedded into CPOE and e-Prescribing tools is Clinical Decision Support (CDS); when the CDS tool identifies a potential conflict, it alerts the provider that his or her order may not align with best practices or the patient's history. There is data that suggests that with such features, EHRs do reduce adverse drug effects significantly.

Interoperability

HIMSS defines interoperability as "the ability of health information systems to work together within and across organizational boundaries in order to advance the effective delivery of healthcare for individuals and communities." The motivation behind this objective to to make sure that patient information and histories are complete at point of care and thereby reduce errors and costs. The longer, larger goal is to have a national Health Information Exhchange (HIE). To meet this objective, EHRs must be able to share their information with other software systems.

Patient Electronic Access

This objective requires that patients be able to view their health information online, download it and share it with a third party—all in a timely manner after their visit. This objective is met through a patient portal—a feature of many EHRs today. Patient portals will also typically allow patients to securely send messages to their doctors, schedule appointments and provide required information. Patient portals may also have other features, such as allowing the request of prescription refills.

Important EHR Considerations

There are several important considerations that every practice should take into account when purchasing an EHR. Leaving these out of the planning process frequently leads to 'bad fits' and frustration with new EHR systems.

Specialist vs Primary Care

Specialists typically don't need all of the charting features that primary care physicians do. Having an EHR with specific templates for your

specialty will allow you to work much more efficiently.
Fortunately, the number of specialties catered to by
the major EHR vendors is expanding rapidly.

Cloud vs. On-Premise

Traditional EHR systems have been based
on on-premise servers. Today, practices can also
access EHR software though the cloud, as
Software-As-A-Service (SAAS).   Cloud-based
EHR software is typically offered on a subscription
model and includes secure data back-up in the
cloud hosting environment. On-premise EHR
systems typically require a greater up-front cost
and more work for on-site implementation, but can
allow for more customization. For many small
practices with limited budgets, cloud based EHR
software can make the transition to EHRs less
financially daunting.

Practice Size

It's not one-size fits all with EHRs. Smaller
practices have different needs than larger practices.
Many EHR vendors will offer different versions of their
software for different practice sizes. Make sure you're
selecting software appropriate for the size of your
practice.

Diagnostic Interfaces

How does your EHR integrate digital data from diagnostic equipment? Is it compatible with the brands of devices you're currently using? Being able to incorporate data from diagnostic equipment and lab reports is critical for maintaining comprehensive patient records. Having an EHR system that does so seamlessly and automatically can save time and reduce errors.

Billing And Practice Management

Submitting billing electronically is a component of Meaningful Use. Many EHR software systems now include billing and practice management components as options. For many practices, these can be attractive features because it makes data entry and claims submission more efficient and less time-consuming.

Disclosure Tracking

Your EHR system should track the disclosures of ePHI and allow you to access these records easily. It's an important safeguard to have in place for managing patient data and remaining HIPAA-compliant.

View Options

The way data is displayed in an EHR is an
important consideration when thinking about ease
of use. We all know certain software is user-
friendly and certain software is not, even though
they both do the same task or provide the same
information. Are you comfortable with how the
patient summary screen displays information?
Are their different options for displaying that
information? Are you able to view patient records
arrayed based on outstanding procedures or
diagnosis? Give some thought as to the
information that your practice needs access to
and how your potential EHR gives you that
information.

Referral Management

It's important for many practices (especially
primary care practices) to be able to track
referrals to outside specialists. Make sure your
EHR offers this ability, including allowing your
system to receive patient reports from these
outside providers. This capability can really
reduce wasted time.

Try It Out!

Finally, it's critical that providers and their
teams actually try their EHR software before they
invest it. Don't simply allow a vendor to offer a
demo either. Have a list of common tasks at your
practice that will need to be done regularly and
make sure you're comfortable completing those
tasks in your selected EHR.

Ch.4 HIPAA

The Health Insurance Portability and Accountability Act (HIPAA) of 1996—including significant changes to it made in ARRA in 2009 — governs privacy and security practices regarding healthcare IT. HIPAA requires providers to control the use and disclosure of patients' protected health information (PHI), and in particular, electronic protected health information (ePHI). The relevance and reach of HIPAA in medical practices has expanded significantly in recent years as the proliferation of HIT has meant much more frequent sharing of ePHI.

The U.S. Department of Health & Human Services' (HHS) Office of Civil Rights (OCR) enforces HIPAA privacy regulations. OCR is an acronym that you'll see with frequency in discussions of HIPAA and HIT generally. In January 2013, OCR published the final "HIPAA Omnibus Rule" regarding updates to HIPAA from ARRA and the Genetic Information Nondiscrimination Act (GINA). Enforcement of these provisions by OCR began on September 23, 2013.

Safeguards

HIPAA is essentially focused on maintaining the privacy and trust of patients that providers have always adhered to. However, it's important that every practice have a formal plan and practices in place for HIPAA compliance, as some of the specific requirements are not self-evident or necessarily obvious, and the penalties and liabilities surrounding HIPAA have also increased. The Breach Notification Rule also requires providers to notify affected patients, HHS and sometimes the media if they discover a breach and the exposure of unencrypted ePHI—so there can also be a cost to a practice's reputation for violating HIPAA technology provisions.

HIPAA regulations are the federally mandated requirements regarding privacy and security and override state laws in most cases. However, if individual states have additional, more stringent privacy and security requirements, those will take precedence over HIPAA.

The HIPAA Security Rule requires covered entities to implement 'administrative, technical and physical safeguards' to ensure the privacy, security and availability of ePHI. The Security

Rule and the Privacy Rule often get confused. While the Privacy Rule pertains to all PHI, the Security Rule focuses exclusively on ePHI—it does not apply to PHI transmitted in paper or orally.

HIPAA regulations are divided into those that are 'required' and those that are 'addressable.' The idea behind this division is to provide some flexibility for providers based on the size of their practices and available resources. If a provider chooses not to implement an 'addressable' standard or implements an alternative to that standard, the decision must be documented. Cost alone cannot be the rationale for non-adoption of an addressable standard.

The starting point for HIPAA security compliance is conducting a risk assessment which is also a Core Objective in achieving meaningful use. Providers must first identify where ePHI is located in their practice and if any such ePHI is vulnerable to breach. After initial protocols and updates are implemented to address identified shortcomings or 'gaps' in security, risk assessments should still be conducted on a regular basis.

The necessary administrative safeguards for HIPAA security compliance include tracking of security incidents (along with documented procedures for dealing with incidents that limit adverse effects), appointment of a practice security officer, ongoing training for staff members

in security protocols (including policies for
computer workstation access and destroying
media with ePHI after use), implementing
penalties for staff members who violate security
protocols (and documenting such incidents),
implementing data back-up plans and business
continuity procedures and conducting regular
reviews of security compliance.

Some of the technical safeguards required by
HIPAA include management of unique software
access identities and log-in credentials (access
management), maintaining audit logs of all
systems that use ePHI, establishing procedures
for both protecting ePHI from alteration and
destruction and identifying those seeking access
to ePHI. Encryption is an 'addressable' technical
standard, but it is highly recommended as a
technical safeguard for all practices.

All security compliance efforts need to be
documented.

OCR Audits

OCR is required to conduct audits of
covered entities. And since the passage of
ARRA, the frequency of these audits has
increased. However, if prudent efforts are being
made to comply with HIPAA technology mandates,
there's no need to fear these audits. Further,

what these audits are looking for is not a mystery. The complete OCR audit protocol can be found on its website.

Breach Notification

The final HIPAA Omnibus Rule updated the requirements for notification in case of a security breach. Patients are required to be notified of any breach of unsecured data; instances involving more than 500 patients require also notifying HHS, which will post the name of the practice on its website. In certain of these cases, the local media will also be alerted. Breaches are now presumed to be reportable unless an analysis shows a low chance that ePHI was revealed. OCR provides guidelines for conducting such an analysis, which can be completed 'in-house' by a medical practice. *Compromised ePHI that is encrypted is not subject to breach notification requirements.*

Encryption

Encryption is one of the central elements of securing ePHI. Some examples of different encryption algorithms include RSA, AES, DES, and Triple-DES/3DES. Different algorithms use different keys. While traditional encryption used

private keys for both encrypting and decrypting
material, some newer encryption algorithms are
'public-key' and use a publicly available key to
encrypt data and require a private key to decrypt
it. Data can –and should be-- encrypted both at
rest and in transit. Any and all data on your
computer can be encrypted—and any programs
and files containing ePHI or administering ePHI
should be encrypted. In practice, very nearly all
communications and data in a modern practice
should be encrypted. (Though you're not required
to do so by HIPAA, your emails should be
encrypted as well.) ePHI shared on the internet
via patient portals also needs to be encrypted.
All patient portal software solutions and EMR
solutions will be encrypted and an IT provider can
work with you to make sure your computer
systems are encrypted.

Penalties

The HITECH ACT mandated both civil and
criminal penalties be levied by HHS for HIPAA
violations. Civil penalties can range from $100
per violation to $50,000 per violation, up to a
maximum of $1.5 million per year. The variance in
penalties depends on the level of knowledge of
the provider (and what they should have known)
about whether they were violation HIPAA, whether
they willfully neglected HIPAA standards, the
amount of damage caused and whether they've

worked to redress that damage. It's important to
note that only in cases of willful neglect can a
penalty be imposed if the violation is corrected
within 30 days. Criminal penalties can be brought
for covered entities and others that knowingly
obtain or disclose ePHI.

Ch.5 Data Back-Up

Having a data back-up and disaster recovery solution for your practice is essential. A disaster recovery plan is required under HIPAA to ensure access to ePHI and it allows your practice to continue functioning in the case of a disaster. Today, it really is like an essential form of practice insurance. What would the cost be in liability, lost productivity and simply lost records if you were to get caught without one?

Perhaps your response is that the likelihood of a disaster striking your practice is low. Well, that depends on what we're thinking of when we talk about disasters. Disasters that disrupt networks and destroy electronic records usually aren't hurricanes, tornadoes or floods. They're much more likely to be mundane accidents like coffee spilled on a computer or a small fire from a connection overheating in the server closet or a sprinkler system errantly turning on or an employee error. Network disasters are much more common than natural disasters. In general, the world of business owners who are considering

back-up and disaster recovery can be divided into
those who have experienced a data loss and
those who haven't. Don't wait to be in the former
category to take care of this essential planning.

Cloud-Based Back-Up

So let's talk about what you should be
considering when implementing a back-up and
disaster recovery solution. First, you want to be
backing up your data and network in the cloud.
You may use a hybrid solution, which backs up
your data on both an on-premise hard drive and
the cloud, but the cloud should definitely be a part
of your solution. Why? Because the cloud
actually affords you more security than on-
premise or local solutions. I know that for many
business owners, this seems odd. Keeping the
data on-site, close-by intuitively seems to be the
more secure solution. But consider where your
data is residing when it's in 'the cloud'. It is
actually going to the highly secure, redundant
data centers of major technology vendors.

These data centers are designed to secure
electronic data—from the technology used to the
physical design of the building to the personnel.
The data that resides in them is encrypted and it
is also encrypted in transit to these data centers.

These centers meet HIPAA and other safety standards. In short, they provide more secure situations for data than residing in a medical practice.

RTO, RPO and Fail-Over

Current cloud back-up solutions do not simply copy your data either. They are managed software solutions that have web-based portals that allow for testing and monitoring and provide alerts if there are issues with backing-up the data. These solutions are often monitored by the practice's outsourced IT partner. Modern data back-up solutions also allow you to control how frequently your data is backed up (for example, every 24 hours, every six hours, every 15 minutes...) and how quickly you can recover that data. These two measures are known as Recovery Point Objective (RPO) and Recovery Time Objective (RTO), respectively. Cloud based data back-up solutions can also allow your team to keep working through a network disaster, by replicating your network in the cloud and providing fail-over operability there. So long as internet access is still available, all workstations, software and processes can be accessed in the cloud in real time.

In talking about cloud-based back-up solutions, it's important to note that many leading EHR and practice management solutions are now cloud-based SAAS software systems and that these vendors should (and almost always do) provide secure, compliant, cloud-based back-up of that data. For practices using such cloud-based systems, data back-up solutions for applications, data and hardware residing outside the EHR system is still a critical need. Part of this implementation will be identifying mission-critical systems and applications.

Personnel Practices

Outside of the technology safeguards that need to be implemented to back-up your data in case of a disaster, there should also be appropriate staff procedures in place for such an event. Does everybody on staff know what to do in case of a disaster? Do they know how to use the technology appropriately in such a situation and what the technology back-up solution is? These are important considerations that should be part of regular planning and training.

Ch. 6 Mobile and BYOD

The rise of mobile computing has spread across all business environments. The practice of letting employees Bring Your Own Device (BYOD) has proliferated for a number of reasons. Employees are using their personal mobile phones and tablets throughout their days for managing all of their life's communications and activities and it make sense that they want to use that same device for their business activities as well. From a convenience and time-efficiency perspective, it's easier to carry around one all-purpose device than it is to carry around a work device and a portable device and switch off between the two for different activities. Also, many users are passionate about the particular device they use—be it an Android device, iPhone, iPad or Windows phone or tablet. These employees simply don't want to be told they have to use a different brand of device that they don't prefer. Forcing employees to use a business-issued mobile device can actually be a hiring deterrent in some situations. Finally, though it presents management challenges from an IT perspective, BYOD allows businesses to save money by not having to purchase mobile devices for employees and, in some cases, by being able to avoid investing in desktops.

These same conveniences and cost-savings occur in medical practices, where busy providers and staff are able to access patient data and communications via their own mobile devices. Many providers recognize that they will increasingly be accessing electronic data when interacting with patients and simply prefer to do so on a tablet rather than using a desktop. And many of the leading EHR software solutions are designed to work on the smaller screens of mobile devices. This use of mobile computing in healthcare delivery is sometimes referred to as mHealth. Whether it's called BYOD, mHealth or simply 'mobile', there is wide consensus that the use of mobile devices in medical practices is here to stay. And though mobile devices need to be managed intelligently, there is no reason why medical practices should fear this development or shy away from taking advantage of the benefits mobile can afford.

HIPAA Compliance And Mobile Devices

As the use of computers and electronic healthcare records grows overall, so too does the use of mobile devices in practices. This use presents a number of manageable security challenges that need to be addressed in order to maintain HIPAA compliance. Unfortunately, in many practices today this necessary security planning has not been done. Some of this oversight comes from the misconception (prevalent in all industries) that security breaches are rare occurrences. The data belies this misconception—security threats should be viewed as daily occurrences to be regularly managed. The other major reason for this oversight is more particular to healthcare—while many industries transitioned to electronic records and heavy use of computers years ago, healthcare has seen the rapid adoption of electronic records over the last few years. It has only been natural that users of these records adapt by accessing them as they do much other electronic data—with their mobile devices. So the usage of mobile in medicine has been more of an unplanned response to a changing work environment and has not been prioritized for effective management and planning.

This gap needs to be addressed as part of risk and security management if it has not been already. HIPAA does not specify mobile or desktop computers—its provisions are applicable across all devices used to access protected health information. HIPAA uses the language of 'workstations' when describing necessary security standards, and workstations in this context can mean phones, tablets, desktops (or even wearable devices). As we have seen previously,

HIPAA requires that there be safeguards around all workstations to restrict unauthorized access. HIPAA also has language covering the tracking and usage of media and devices containing patient information. In short, this means mobile devices must be restricted appropriately.

HIPAA requires that the location of devices with ePHI be tracked continuously. Obviously, in situations where people are using their personal devices, this presents serious challenges. The answer is simply not to have protected data residing in your mobile device. Mobile devices should act more like remote desktops—they should access protected data that resides in your practice's network or in the cloud, but they should not be saving that data directly in the device. The data should remain within the servers that are already secured and HIPAA compliant. This also means that work-related data is accessed entirely separately from the personal data that is also accessed (or stored) on these mobile devices. This is a critical consideration—ePHI and employees' personal data should not be intermingling.

Mobile Device Management

One of the options that practices have is to implement mobile device management (MDM) software. MDM software has developed over the

last few years to allow organizations to centrally
manage mobile devices through a central hub in
their network (or via a cloud-based hub). This can
be managed by either an internal IT staff or an IT
services partner. MDM software grants certain
controls over employees' mobile devices to the
organization—typically including access control,
security and encryption settings and control over
processes in the event of loss or theft. Therefore,
employees must consent to this control of their
devices and it's important to define clearly what
your MDM software will manage. It is also worth
considering what the policy will be for employees
who do not consent to participating in MDM
management.

Access Control

Access Control Lists (ACLs) or role-based
log-in management allows practices to define
what applications or databases an employee
using a mobile device can access and what
permissions they have for what they can do once
access is granted. For instance, controls can be
set to not allow certain users to delete any data.

Remote Wipes

Even if strong efforts are made to ensure that no ePHI resides on mobile devices, there is still the possibility of that data residing on mobile devices. If a mobile device is lost or stolen, MDM software will allow auto-locking of the device by the IT administrator from the central control hub, which will require a long password to be entered for anybody wishing to access the device. In many cases, you'll actually want to 'wipe' all of the data off of the device to be completely safe. Again, this can be done remotely—and the policy regarding when this will be implemented should be clear for all BYOD employees since it involves their personal devices. It's also important to have a clear theft or loss reporting process in place that every employee is aware of so that these incidents can be dealt with as quickly as possible.

End-of-Life Policy

It's also important that in BYOD environments, there are policies in place for when employees want to get rid of their personal devices (usually to replace them with newer models). Again, the possibility remains that ePHI and other sensitive data is now on these devices and theft of data from discarded devices does indeed occur. Appropriate disposal policies

should be in place so that this data cannot be
retrieved by any motivated criminal.

Maintaining Appropriate Security Practices

It's important that there be clearly defined
and written rules regarding mobile security
practices for every member of the practice and
that these practices be reviewed regularly. One of
the ways that practices can get into trouble is by
having the appropriate technological safeguards
in place, but then having employees bypass these
safeguards either out of lack of awareness or just
laziness and lack of prioritization in the midst of
getting things done every day.   Does everybody
at your practice know that it is unacceptable to
send text messages with ePHI? This is just one
of many protocols that need to be enshrined
regarding mobile. Fortunately, any
comprehensive HIPAA risk assessment—which
should be scheduled regularly-- will cover mobile
as well. Technology safeguards and policy
compliance by employees are the key to real
security with mobile.

Healthcare And Technology Today: A Guide for Providers and
Practice Managers

Ch. 7 Websites

It goes without saying (or should!) that your
medical practice needs a high-quality website
today. Websites establish your credibility and
your brand and provide necessary information for
prospective patients looking for a provider.
Websites can also allow you to communicate
information to your target patient population and
be found more easily by prospective patients.
The experience that you provide digital visitors to
your website should match the experience you
provide patients who come to your office. So
what is required to provide an excellent website
experience? Let's review some of the major items
you should keep in mind.

Patient Portals and Security

Your website is not your patient portal. I
know this may be a confusing point for everybody
who has visited a great medical practice website

and seen the patient portal right there.   So what
do I mean when I say your website is not your
patient portal?   Quite simply, they're two different
systems, even though they may present to the
website visitor as an integrated whole.   Your
patient portal will be part of your HER software
system. Even though access to the patient portal
will be (and should be) easily located on your
website for existing patients, once a visitor signs
into that patient portal, he or she has left your
website and accessed the encrypted and secure
hosting environment of your EHR system. This is
a different environment than your website. This
distinction is critical for security management. On
your website and its hosting environment, you are
not sharing ePHI. Your website is simply sharing
public information about your website and medical
topics that can be accessed by anybody. This
means that you are not responsible for making
sure your website meets HIPAA encryption and
security requirements. So, in designing and
managing your website, you need only meet the
standards of any other informational business
website and can (and should) avoid the costs of
developing a highly secure environment for
protected communication with patients.

Content Management System

　　Your website should feature a Content
Management System (CMS). A CMS allows any

designated team members to access the back-end
of the website in order to be able to easily add
and edit fresh content, including text, video and
pictures.   If needed, various levels of access and
activity can be designated to different team
members. (Again, ePHI and other sensitive data
does not reside in your website CMS.) You
specifically do not need to have any coding ability
to be able to use a CMS—these systems are
designed for non-technical people. The firm that
designs and builds your website should give you
some basic training on using the CMS when the
website becomes operational.

A CMS is a critical component for a
successful, modern website. It is important that
you be able to regularly provide updated
information on your website without having to call
on your web development team every time you
wish to do so. Adding blog posts and up-to-date
practice information allows visitors to see that
your practice is vibrant and active and is an
important part of branding and establishing trust
online today.   This current information is also
important for search engines in assigning
authority to your website.   The major software
platforms for publishing websites today will all
feature a CMS. We recommend the WordPress
platform to most of our clients—it is easy to use
and easily indexed by Google.

Blog

Your website should have a blog that allows you to publish posts. As we mentioned above, publishing regular, useful, relevant content for your visitors is important not only for branding and engagement, but also important for search engines in ranking your website.   Your website should be designed to have your latest blog posts (or at least snippets of them) integrated into the layout of your homepage.

Responsive Design

The majority of visitors today to local business websites—including medical practices—visit them via mobile devices. This percentage will only increase in the coming years.   Your website needs to be designed to be user-friendly not only on larger desktop screens, but also on the smaller screens of tablets and mobile phones. 'Responsive' design refers to designing your website to automatically adjust its layout, spacing and sizing when accessed on smaller screens so that it provides a great user-experience on these devices.   It's not necessary to have separate mobile and desktop websites. Your single website should be designed responsively to work across devices.

Social Media Integration

Your website should feature buttons linking to the social media sites your practice actively manages and participates on. These buttons, when clicked, should open in separate browser windows. If you don't actively participate in a certain social media platform, don't include it in your website design.

Visitor Engagement

Your website is often the first interaction prospective patients will have with your practice. How does it represent your practice? Does it reflect your brand? Your design should be customized to reflect your practice. Your design should also be something you and your team are proud of and excited about. No matter your design, your website should feature bold, engaging photography of your practice. Relying on stock photography will give your website a cold, generic feel.

Your website design should also reflect what you want it to achieve. Are you looking for prospective patients to be able to easily contact you? Direct them clearly where to go to get in touch with big, bright buttons. Are you looking to provide excellent educational information to your target audience? Again, allow visitors to know

clearly where to access that information. People
online have short attention spans. Don't make the
error of assuming that they understand what to do
or where to go or that they'll take the time to
figure it out. Make things clear and easy for your
visitors.

Ch. 8 Digital Marketing

Today, digital marketing provides an important (and growing) avenue for attracting new patients. Many patients start their treatment paths online, by researching ailments, treatments and doctors. According to Pew Research, 47% of internet users search for information about doctors online. According to Google, 77% of patients used search before scheduling an appointment online. Having your practice be easily found online can be very valuable. Let's take a look at some of the options you have in online marketing.

SEO

Search Engine Optimization (SEO) is the practice of increasing your website's rankings in search engines for relevant terms and increasing overall traffic to your site.   The type of traffic that is increased through SEO is referred to as organic traffic. (Organic traffic is distinct from paid traffic, which we'll address below.) Most practices (and businesses in general) will outsource SEO to an agency, as successfully managing SEO requires time and expertise that aren't normally available.

The first step in any SEO campaign is to make sure that you're targeting the appropriate keywords. Google accounts for the vast majority of online search and is the main search engine that any SEO campaign will focus on (even though, generally speaking, these same efforts will result in rankings improvements in the other search engines as well). Google publishes the monthly search traffic data for each 'keyword' or term people search for. You, or more likely your SEO firm, will use this data as the basis for creating the list of terms you'll target in your campaign.

SEO does not involve making any payments to Google or any other search engine. Rather, it involves a variety of activities designed to make Google's automated search algorithm rank your site higher for certain terms. Historically (and still, unfortunately, today), there are many SEO firms that will 'guarantee' first-place rankings or 'guarantee' results in a very short time period and for the same fee, no matter what business you are in. No reputable SEO firm will make such guarantees, because ultimately the SEO firm does not control Google's ranking algorithm. SEO is a long-term process that typically takes several months, at minimum, to begin showing positive results. Based on experience and expertise, an SEO firm will engage in practices such as on-site

optimization, content creation, link-building,
coding optimization and site speed enhancement
and making sure the user experience is designed
well and maintained.

SEO, when conducted by a reputable firm, is
usually a very good marketing strategy in terms of
ROI. The reason for this is that it specifically
targets potential patients at the moment they are
searching for terms related to your practice.
When looked at in the larger context of all
marketing, SEO is the only avenue that provides
the ability for businesses to be directly in front of
a potential customer at the very moment they are
actively looking for your services. (This,
fundamentally, is why Google is such an
enormously successful business.)   Most SEO
campaigns are billed at a flat monthly rate. As
your SEO campaign progresses, your rankings
and traffic to your site will increase, but your flat
rate of cost will remain consistent. If a campaign
has been planned effectively based on calculated
values of new patients and realistic expectations
of traffic and conversions based on available data
and experience, this is when an SEO campaign
should become consistently profitable.

Content Marketing

Content marketing is a necessary part of SEO today and also a practice that can stand on its own as a marketing strategy. Content marketing involves publishing content online—be it audio, video, text or a combination of all three. Content marketing, when done effectively, accomplishes a number of goals. From an SEO perspective, it can help with link-building and rankings. Great pieces of content can garner visitors on their own and be listed directly in search results. Content also positions your practice as an authority in your specialty area and the tone of your content can reflect your personality and the brand of your practice. Content can be published on your website's blog and that same content can also be published in social media channels. It's important that the content your practice produces be original content.

Paid Advertising

Paid advertising online involves payment to search engines (and possibly other networks) for placement of digital ads in targeted areas. These ads can be 'banner' ads placed in online publications or they can be simple text ads that appear next to search results. Increasingly, there are also opportunities for video ads online.

When working with paid ads, it's important to understand what you're paying for. You are paying for every click on your ad (Pay-Per-Click, or PPC), which then leads that visitor to a designated 'landing' page on your website. Whether that visitor then 'converts' by either contacting you via your website or by phone has no impact on what you pay for the advertising. Paid advertising works at the top of the marketing funnel. It's therefore very important to collect data on what ads are actually leading to conversions and, ultimately, patients. There are also a number of factors involved in working with the search engines and their bidding systems for pricing and placing ads. To make sure a paid digital campaign is effective and that the money spent is managed efficiently, it's often helpful to have a digital agency manage the campaign. This process is involved enough that there are specialists who just focus on managing PPC campaigns. Normally, the agency that runs your SEO campaign will also be able to run your PPC campaign.

Social Media

Social media, is increasingly important in digital marketing. Social media engagement is (one of many) ranking factors in SEO. But more importantly, social media can allow practices (through doctors and staff) to educate and engage the public, allow providers and other professionals to network and can increase the visibility of a practice.

There are two primary risks in social media for medical practices. The first is that the very informal nature of social media can allow for opportunities for communication that undermine the professional stature of a practice. The second major risk is that a HIPAA violation will occur inadvertently. There is no regulation against sharing 'de-identified' medical information on social media. Giving patient advice over social media is generally not a good idea. Your practice should have clear, written rules regarding social media participation. It's also a good idea to preserve all communications on social media for auditing purposes.

Social media, in all its evolving forms, is here to stay and will only grow in importance over the next several years. The answer is not to shy away from it, but to embrace it and participate smartly.

Digital Marketing Going Forward

Digital marketing is attractive to medical practices because it is, in general, a highly trackable marketing arena that is gaining more and more users every year. As new avenues

develop in digital, there will be new opportunities
for engagement with prospective patients as well
as the necessity for adjusting strategies.
Whatever changes are to come, however, the
basic fact remains that more and more people will
continue to find their providers electronically.

Healthcare And Technology Today: A Guide for Providers and
Practice Managers

Ch.9 Outsourcing IT

Many medical practices choose to work with an outsourced IT partner to manage their technology needs rather than trying to handle these obligations in-house. In this chapter, we'll take a look at some of the reasons medical practices choose this route and some of the considerations to keep in mind when doing so.

Managed Services

Medical practices will generally choose to work with a Managed Services Provider (MSP). MSPs are IT firms that provide managed services. What are managed services? Managed services are outsourced IT support and consultation services that are contracted with set (usually monthly) costs. The alternative to managed services traditionally has been 'break-fix' service. When some piece of your technology breaks, a technician is called to come fix it. There are a few disadvantages to the break-fix approach. The first is that it obviously requires that something break before anything happens. This can

translate into significant costs: replacing broken
hardware, possible lost data, lost productivity,
dissatisfied patients, damage to the practice's brand,
and the time of the IT professionals who need to be
on-site to fix things.   The break-fix approach can also
result in unexpected and unpredictable IT costs.

Because of all these drawbacks, over the last several
years, the managed services model has become
extremely popular.   It can provide not only more
predictable (and ultimately, often reduced) costs, but
also the ability to manage technology pro-actively
through remote monitoring. The advent of high-speed
internet connections allows MSPs to install small
pieces of software in the computers and networks of
their clients that allow their technicians to become
aware of possible issues and resolve them remotely
before anything actually 'breaks' and disrupts
processes at the medical practice. Remote
monitoring therefore allows for reductions in on-site
time.

Different MSPs will have different packages that
include different services—not all managed services
offerings are created equal. Additionally, many MSPs
will tailor custom solutions for their clients, depending
on their specific needs. Let's take a look at some of
the most common features of managed services
offerings.

Help Desk Support

Many managed services packages will include
help-desk support, either during business hours or
24/7, depending on the client's needs. Help-desk
support is useful for all of the normal technology
questions and bugs that arise during the course of
doing business that eat into productivity and valuable
employee time. Why is my email not opening? My
Excel spreadsheet has frozen! Having a help desk
that is staffed by qualified technicians to deal with all
of these issues can be a great asset for a practice.
You want to make sure that your MSP's help-desk is
staffed by certified professionals. You'll also want to
ask what the normal response time is to calls.
Additionally, the help desk technician might be able to
log-in remotely (if provided permission) to resolve
issues.

On-Site Support

The majority of issues will be able to be
resolved by either the help-desk or through pro-active
resolution through remote monitoring before they
even become an 'issue.' For those issues that can't
be resolved remotely, many MSP packages will offer
an on-site support component. Depending on the
needs of the practice, certain guarantees for
response-time and availability are often included.

Remote Monitoring

Remote monitoring, as we've mentioned, can identify issues and allow for resolution before they cause disruptions. Remote monitoring also normally includes security management, including updating anti-malware and anti-virus software and installing security patches for installed software. Maintaining such updates is a critical component of HIPAA compliance.

Data Back-Up and Recovery

Today, many managed services offerings also include data back-up and business recovery solutions.

Vendor Management

Outsourcing IT support also gives practices the advantage of having a partner to manage relationships with technology vendors and make sure they are delivering as promised. Often, technology firms will have existing relationships with these technology vendors and be familiar with their practices and solutions.

HIPAA Management

Your outsourced IT partner should also play an integral role in your practice's HIPAA compliance management. Many IT partners will provide dedicated solutions designed specifically to monitor HIPAA status and make compliance tracking easier. Your IT partner will need to sign a Business Associate Agreement with you, which specifies that they will act in a HIPAA-compliant manner as well.

Outsourcing IT services often allows medical practices to access IT experience and talent that would be prohibitively costly or time-consuming to bring on 'in-house.'

Ch.10 Ransomware

Unfortunately today, we cannot talk about healthcare IT without talking about ransomware. Ransomware sounds scary. It evokes the image from the movies we all know of a kidnapping and a ransom note written in letters cut out from different magazines.

Ransomware is actually scary. It's a type of malware that holds your data (and sometimes your network and even identity) hostage by encrypting it until you pay the author of the malware to 'release' your data by providing a decryption key. There's often a threat that your data will be destroyed in periodic installments if you don't pay. So, like kidnappings for ransom in the real world, the motivation is to make money.

Ransomware in various forms has been around since the 1980s, but it really came to the public's attention starting in September 2013 when the ransomware CryptoLocker began holding Windows computers in the US hostage using Bitcoin digital currency to collect the ransom payments. CryptoLocker was eventually solved by an international police operation, but successors, like CryptoWall, have taken its place. CryptoWall has driven an estimated 325 million dollars in ransom payments.

Ransomware is the most prevalent cybersecurity threat facing businesses in all industries today. According the to the cybersecurity software firm Symantec, in 2015, 362,000 new variants of ransomware were identified. The FBI has reported that damages from ransomware attacks in the first quarter of 2016 were $200 million, up from the $24 million for all of 2015. And healthcare providers are an especially attractive target for ransomware attacks because of the sensitive and up-to-date information contained in their data files as well as the fact that inaccessibility to certain software and processes in healthcare can be extremely costly both from a financial and patient safety perspective. If you are a kidnapper, it makes sense to go after valuable hostages. According to another report by cybersecurity software firm Websense, healthcare providers are 4.5 times more likely to face a CryptoWall attack than other types of businesses.

How Does A Ransomware Attack Happen?

Ransomware usually accesses a computer or network through predictable avenues: phishing

emails, unpatched software programs, software
downloads, malicious websites or
'malvertisements'—infected advertisements that
on legitimate websites that can be infectious when
clicked on.

In the context of ransomware, phishing emails are
attempts by cybercriminals to get employees to
download ransomware onto their computer and
network. 99% of all ransomware attacks are
initiated through email.

Phishing emails can usually be identified by some
characteristic features. Phishing emails often
contain links directly in the email message. In
particular, they can often have links that lead
directly to '.exe' files. Phishing emails will often
try to appear as though they're coming from a
major company. Often a major tech company, like
Google, Microsoft or Facebook. They may even
be associated with fake websites that look similar
to the major company's website. These emails
also often contain threats or urgent calls to action,
suggesting there's been irregular activity in your
account and it will be closed if you don't act *now*.

Whether coming from a phishing email or some
other source, once the ransomware has infected a
computer it will begin encrypting the files on that
computer. The most common form of encryption
used in webmail is RSA 2048, which is effectively
impenetrable without a decryption key.
Ransomware will not just encrypt files on the

computer it was downloaded onto; it will spread
across the network and encrypt files throughout
the practice. The net effect is that one accidental
download of ransomware by a team member can
quickly encrypt all of the files across a network.

Once at least some the files are encrypted, the
cybercriminals will display a screen on your
computer or a link to a website notifying you that
you've been attacked. Unlike some other types of
hacking attacks, ransomware only profits the
criminals when the victim is aware that they've
been attacked. This page will have the 'ransom
note.' It will usually include a deadline for making
a payment (usually through the e-currency
Bitcoin), along with instructions for making the
payment.   It will also often have a threat that the
encrypted data will be destroyed if the ransom
payment is not made. If the ransom is paid, the
hackers promise to provide decryption software.

How to Respond to An Attack

If you are attacked, it is possible that the
ransomware being used is a recognizable variant
and there may be the possibility of decrypting your
data. Outside of this scenario, if there is no data
back-up to access, the only option becomes
paying the ransom to retrieve the data—a route
followed by many victims.

Security Measures

Many practices become attentive to
preventative measures after they've been
attacked. Don't wait for that to happen. There
are definite steps your practice can start taking
today to not only lessen the chances of falling
victim to a ransomware attack, but also
decreasing the negative impact of an attack.

The single most important step that you can take
is to have an effective, regularly tested data back-
up and business continuity solution in place. If
your practice's data is being backed up regularly
and securely and that data can be retrieved and
accessed quickly, ransomware does not pose a
threat to you. Even if your data on your network
is encrypted, you can retrieve your back-ups of
that data from their remote location.

Make sure that you have up-to-date anti-malware
and anti-virus solutions installed on all of the
endpoints in your network. Also make sure that
security patches are installed and up-to-date for
your software. (These are regular maintenance
services that an MSP will usually provide as part
of a managed services solution.) Intelligently
limiting user access to only needed areas of the
network can also play a role in limiting the files
that are encrypted should a ransomware attack
happen.

It's also critical that everybody at the practice
knows how to identify phishing emails and is
reminded regularly to be wary of unsolicited email.
Nobody should ever click on a link in an
unsolicited email—there's no reason to do it. If
you do receive an unsolicited email and you're
unsure if it's legitimate and from a business that
you deal with, simply call up that business that
appears to be sending the email.

Glossary

AHIMA

The American Health Information Management Association (AHIMA) is a nonprofit organization that plays a leading role in pushing the adoption of EHRs.

The Breach Notification Rule

The HIPAA Breach Notification Rule requires practices to notify affected individuals and HHS in case of a data breach. In some instances, local media will also need to be notified.

BYOD

Bring-Your-Own-Device (BYOD) is the practice of having employees use their own mobile devices for company computing tasks.

Cloud Computing

Cloud computing is internet-based computing that allows individuals and businesses to access shared computer resources at remote hosting locations. Cloud computing gives the ability to access hardware and software on demand, without investing in on-premise architecture.

Content Management System (CMS)

A back-end administration area of a website that allows users to easily update content on a website without having to know how to code.

Core Objectives

The ten standards for Stage 2 of Meaningful Use.

EHR

An electronic health record (also sometimes referred to as an EMR, or electronic medical record) refers to both the electronic record of a specific patient as well as to the software systems that support those records.

ePHI

Electronic Protected Health Information (ePHI) refers to any electronic protected health information (PHI) that is covered under HIPAA.

HIMSS

The Healthcare Information and Management Systems Society (HIMSS) is a global nonprofit focused on HIT. HIMSS is a thought leader on HIT.

HIPAA

The federal Health Insurance Portability and Accountability Act of 1996.

HIPAA Omnibus Rule

The final "HIPAA Omnibus Rule" was published in January 2013 regarding updates to HIPAA from ARRA and the Genetic Information Nondiscrimination Act (GINA). Enforcement of these provisions by OCR began on September 23, 2013.

HIPAA Privacy Rule

The HIPAA Privacy Rule went into effect on April 14, 2003. The HIPAA Privacy Rule deals with protecting the privacy of individually identifiable health information, including medical records—protected health information (PHI).

HIPAA Security Rule

The HIPAA Security Rule went into effect on April 21, 2003. Compliance for most covered entities was required by April 21, 2005. While the Privacy Rule covers all protected health information (PHI), the Security Rule specifically deals with electronic protected health information (ePHI).

The HITECH Act

The Health Information Technology for Economic and Clinical Health Act (HITECH) is the $147 billion portion of the American Recovery and Reinvestment Act (ARRA) of 2009 directed toward reimbursing the healthcare industry for the adoption of healthcare IT.

HITPC

The Health IT Policy Committee (HITPC) makes recommendations to ONC on a policy framework for developing and adopting a national infrastructure for exchanging health information.

HITSC

The Health IT Standards Committee (HITSC) makes recommendations to ONC on standards, implementation specifications and certification criteria in the use and exchange of healthcare information and coordinates standards testing.

ICD-10

The International Statistical Classification of Diseases and Related Health Problems: Tenth Revision (ICD-10) is a more expansive and detailed coding system that CMS has required all HIPAA-covered providers to use by October 1, 2015.

MACRA

The Medicare Access and CHIP Reauthorization Act (MACRA) of 2015 applies to providers covered under Medicare Part B. The Act institutes the Merit-Based Incentive Payment System (MIPS).

Malvertisements

Digital advertisements placed by cybercriminals on websites that, when clicked upon, can download malware to a computer and network.

Managed Services Provider (MSP)

An outsourced IT firm providing ongoing IT support services at a fixed priced. Managed

services are a replacement from the older 'break-
fix' model.

Meaningful Use

Meaningful Use is the standard for
effectively adopting healthcare IT that is used by
the Medicare and Medicaid EHR Incentive
Programs. It is also the shorthand term often
used to refer to the Incentive Programs
themselves.

mHealth

The use of mobile computing devices in
healthcare.

Mobile Device Management (MDM)

Mobile Device Management (MDM)
software allows organizations to centrally manage
mobile devices through a central hub in their
network (or via a cloud-based hub).

NCVHS

The National Committee On Vital and
Health Statistics (NCVHS) advises the Secretary
of Health and Human Services on health
information policy and reports to Congress on
HIPAA implementation.

NQF

The National Quality Forum (NQF) is a
nonpartisan nonprofit organization made up of
over 430 member organizations, whose goal is to
improve healthcare in the US. NQF has been
involved in defining standards for meaningful use.

NwHIN

The Nationwide Health Information Network
(NwHIN) is a set of standards and policies
established by ONC to enable the secure
exchange of health information over the Internet.

OCR

The Office of Civil Rights (OCR) is part of
the U.S. Department of Health & Human Services
(HHS) and enforces HIPAA privacy regulations.

Office of the National Coordinator (ONC)

The Office of the National Coordinator for
Health Information Technology, abbreviated ONC,
is a position within the US Department of Health &
Human Services (HHS). The position was created
by Executive Order in 2004 and written into
legislation by the HITECH Act.

Patient Portal

A secure online interface that gives patients
access to their personal health information and
may support activities such as secure email with
providers, scheduling appointments and making
payments. Often included as modules in EHR
systems.

Pay-Per-Click (PPC)

A form of online advertising in which
advertisers pay for every click of their ad. Each

click sends a visitor to a designated page on the advertiser's website.

Phishing Emails

Emails sent by cybercriminals in an attempt to gain access to a business network or to download malicious software to a business network. Phishing emails are the main source of ransomware.

RPO

The recovery point objective (RPO) is a measure in data back-up and recovery and is the maximum period allowed for data to be lost in a disaster.

RTO

The recovery time objective (RTO) is a measure in data back-up and recovery and is the targeted time after a disaster to have a network and data restored to operational.

SaaS

Software-as-a-Service (SaaS) is a cloud-based model for licensing software on a subscription basis.

Search Engine Optimization (SEO)

The practice of increasing your website's rankings in search engines for relevant terms and increasing overall organic traffic to your site.